STORM DANCER

OTHER WORKS BY WAYNE KEON

Sweetgrass (poems, 1972) with Ronald and Orville Keon
Thunderbirds of the Ottawa (a novel, 1977) with Orville Keon
Sweetgrass II (poems, 1990)

STORM DANCER
Poems

WAYNE KEON

The Mercury Press

Copyright © Wayne Keon, 1993

ALL RIGHTS RESERVED. No part of this book may be reproduced by any means without the written permission of the publisher, with the exception of brief passages for review purposes.

The publisher gratefully acknowledges the financial assistance of the Canada Council, the Ontario Arts Council, and the Government of Ontario through the Ontario Publishing Centre.

Editor: Beverley Daurio
Cover design: Gordon Robertson
Cover painting: "Rain Over Water" (1974) by Paterson Ewen
(acrylic on gouged plywood)
Collection of the London Regional Art and Historical Museums, purchased with matching funds from Wintario, 1980
Printed and bound in Canada by Metropole Litho
Composition in Berkeley Book and Gill Sans by TASK

ACKNOWLEDGEMENTS

Poems from *Storm Dancer* have appeared or are forthcoming in:
Acta Victoriana, Antigonish Review, ARC, Beneath the Surface, Breakthrough, Canadian Author and Bookman, Canadian Dimensions, Canadian Literature, Carousel, Dalhousie Review, Dandelion, Gatherings, Green's Magazine, The Moosehead Anthology, NeWest, New Quarterly, Next Exit, Paragraph, Prairie Journal of Canadian Literature, Queen's Quarterly, Tabula Rasa, Toronto South Asia Review,
and in the following anthologies:
Canadian Native Literature in English: An Anthology, edited by Terry Goldie and Daniel David Moses; *There Will Always Be a Sky*, edited by George Swede; *Native Writers and Canadian Writing*, edited by W.H. New.

CANADIAN CATALOGUING IN PUBLICATION:
Keon, Wayne
Storm dancer
Poems.
ISBN 0-920544-97-5
I. Title.
PS8571.E76887 1993   C811'.54   C93-094764-9
PR9199.3.K46S87 1993

The Mercury Press
137 Birmingham Street
Stratford, Ontario
Canada N5A 2T1

to Bertholde

CONTENTS

down to agawa 9
heart nd soul 11
toltec silver 12
crossin the malahat 13
high travellin 15
song for bertholde 16
for sarain stump 17
to teotihaucan 19
beyond survival 22
when i get to run this world 24
breakfast in the nation's capital 27
yucatan sun 29
letter from guernevaca 31
agawa shore 33
south of burrard street 36
sorcery and power 38
another form of art 40
turbines and steel 43
down at college park 45
all the way down 47
willow and lite 49
voices 51
the bell of saint john 54

storm dancer   55
sierra blue   57
suncatcher   58
for w.h. new   60
bein in charge nd all   61
silver and clay   62
nobody sleeps at nite any more   64
yaqui desert   66
just about anything   67
silver and rain   68
proclamations and dust   70
for jeannette   72
rainy days   74
down the fast lane   76
at allison pass   78
earth walk talks   80
Spirit Warrior Raven: Dream Winter   81
Spirit Warrior Raven: Emerald Spring   91
Spirit Warrior Raven: Rainbow Village   97

down to agawa

dancin thru that
old dimension
once

again called
fractured
time

nd space that's really
just the great circle

on the northeast side
of superior
when

yellow nd amber mixed
with orange nd
floatin

along alona bay
hangin near
the top

of that great mountain
great mountain
of mercy
takin

out my sadness
she took my sadness there
with the mist nd the clouds
like ashes comin down
on the wind
thru the pass

to agawa prayin
nd prayin nd raven
divin down
to the bay side of the rock cliff
hearin nothin but the breathin
nd the poundin
between the rocks
nd waves bangin
nd crashin up the canyon
shakin that dull roar all around

nd sacred paintings made
when dimensions meant nothin
nd time meant nothin
nd standin still
soakin in the power nd people of
so long ago

nd carter startin to shake
like that leaf
thrown on the ground
shakin there
in front of me

nd it starts openin up
she saw it openin up
saw it all openin up
that hole in the air
catchin superior days
clothed all
in gold
in gold
nd fine ojibway dust

heart nd soul

when the toltec jaguar man
stood before the council
of priests

no one questioned his bravery
or his strength
no one questioned his honour
or his skill

the offer was unconditional
his heart was ripped
from his chest
cavity
still poundin
nd prayin to the god
he called sun
nd soul
of all his life

toltec silver

watchin those lites
blinkin
along

the hill side in taxco

breath
slippin out into
the air

nd mist comin off her mouth

after the sun's
sunk down
nd

the silver everywhere

flashin in her
eye nd
hand

takin all that heat
nd boilin

toltec heart
poundin
nd carvin
poundin
nd carvin
the silver

long into the night

crossin the malahat

i've given up
on just
about
everything now

my pension
the bureaucrats
nd teachers
who lied to me

ask my lawyer
nd the therapist
nd maybe ask
the priest
who heard my
last confession

they're all in this together

i've given up
on just
about
anything now
just
about

but not the
mountains
nd not the
nootka

the nootka
love
song

i once heard

crossin the
malahat
with
you

high travellin

no shaman
denied that
high up winter
is long

been
almost two
years in the snow now

nd i
never met any
one along the ridge

not many come this way

just the eagle
nd raven

soarin
nd cryin
soarin
nd cryin
soarin
nd cryin

on all that
blue nd
wind

song for bertholde

if
  i had
    a cloud
        nd
          i had
            a dream

i'd turn in the wind

            i'd
              turn to
                your sea

    i'd turn in the wind

                i'd
                  sail in
                    your blue
                nd
            turn down
          a blue sea

      i'd
     turn
  home to you

            but sundown
       sends the nite nd rain
       nd sundown
     brings the blue
  the summer nites
nd candle lites

i'd turn them home to you

for sarain stump

each time i
go down
now

to

mexhico
mexhico
mexhico
mexhico

i call both
of them
in

i mean both the
eagle nd
raven

for that flight home

nd she comes
she comes
screamin
nd cryin
flyin nd
dyin nd
cryin nd
flyin

takin yuh home now boy

clear through that
sierra
sky

she's takin
yuh clear
thru

nd don't worry sarain
this flight
ain't gonna
stop for nothin

cos
eagle don't
know nothin about

no customs
nd nothin about
no border crossings
nd nothin at all
about no time

to teotihaucan

in teotihaucan
there's a
temple

for praying

where you wore
a plume and
a gown

made of quetzal
all bronze
green

and silver

with red on your
mouth and at
dawn

there's moonlight
fastened to
feathers

there's sun

on the breath
of your
hand

and you walk by
the pillar and
toltecs

where jaguar
soldiers
began

i've staggered
behind
the

procession

and followed you
all that i
can

to teotihaucan
power
and

beauty

dragging my heart
in the
sand

to a temple
of conch
shells

and petals

to the temple
where you
had

to lie down

where the sun
and the moon
were

created

where gods
and love
had

to die

where gods and
your love
had to
die

beyond survival

saturday a.m.
i stagger down to the bathroom
groping along the corridor
jesus, i can hardly
get my eyes open
dodging these decepticons
and transformers and crawling
little turtle creatures lurking
just beyond the tooth paste
comic books and spiderman
images everywhere
while he talks to me
endlessly
he thinks i used to live
in the old days
that i'm old fashioned
like my brand new notebook computer
small enough to fit in an eight
and a half by eleven imprint in my briefcase
is outta date or something yet it runs
at 33 MHz has 4KB RAM and an 80MB drive on board
state of the art they told me when they sold it to me
but he says it's old fashioned
only black and white
i don't like
being referred to as a relic
but he says he likes some of my stuff
like the dreamcatchers
hanging everywhere
and medicine wheels on the wall
beside raven and bear and eagle
and smoky mountain images

i'm just remembering last night
you in my arms
naked
except for your socks
pouring that pure white light
directly into my arteries
and exploding
somewhere
somewhere
out there in the dark

this son of mine
calls me back again
what are we having for breakfast
and asks me again if i used to be
a witch doctor back
in the old
days

i
just say
my prayers
praying
and
praying
for strength
only for strength
please give me strength
to last another day
to get awake and alive
and get beyond
a little beyond what she calls
being beyond
survival

when i get to run this world

i won't need
a bureaucracy of thousands
or a mob for the inner cabinet
there'll just
be banjo
and me

at my right side
with four sets of four
desk top cray computers networked
through to each of the hemispheres

by then there'll probably be 986 chips around
the korean kind
that hold about 44 KB's each
and hardware that'll run at 97.3 MHz

we'll rename everyone for openers
give everyone a real name
it shouldn't cause
that much confusion
half the souls
out there don't know who they are
anyway they'll probably
thank us

big job!
nahhhh....banjo'll
probably be able to get it all
directly into RAM

we'll run things
from the sky world
and devote one

of the banks
of computers
to the east
west
south
and north

and one
to each world
of sky
and earth
water
and
underworld

we'll do things the way
the people
used to
long

ago

but i won't be at the command console
in case things get out of control
banjo'll have to handle all
that coaxial networking
and stuff by
himself

i'll be down there
on the yucatan
with
you

with those willow songs
and jaguar dreams
and sun

everywhere

raven
on my
shoulder

dancing
and
dancing
between the
yucatan sand
and the sea

for your love
for your
love

forever
for

your
love

breakfast in the nation's capital

i've got to
purge this
guilt
once
again

in your arms

even though
the Grand Hotel's
not there any more
and the twenty
four
rooms
are gone

i'll settle
for the multi
national conglomerate
sprawled
over the entire city block

and maybe
we could go over
to bank street
when it's all over
and have breakfast
for a buck ninety nine

and maybe
i'll feel better
once i eat
and try not to remember
any of this any more

i mean how the
cree
caribou
up at
fort george
are still
drowning

so that
you
and i
and sean
can stay
alive
in this
great
confederation

yucatan sun

by the
temple
gate

the soldiers
wait

but the eagles
have all
gone

the
courtyard songs
have

all been
sung

my heart's
been
all

undone

on a stone
that's
old

and a game
that's
cold

down
in yucatan
yucatan

down
in yucatan
sun

letter from guernevaca

i could
meet you
in the morelos valley
linda

in the flower
city of
fame

you could
come down
to the zocalo
in a dress of jacaranda

jacaranda
and flame

may is still the best month
here
for the flowers
and i'll tell you about that old mural
down at the palace door

the one where
the eagle and jaguar
warrior
battles
the conquistador

i've got a room
at the palacio
the bed's
brass
antique

i'll probably be here
for a while
in case you think
about comin
down

i'm here every thursday
after seven
and
i'd wait for
you

wait
for
you

past
ten

agawa shore

only the spirits
wander around
at agawa
shore

and i could hardly make it
to the top of the cliff
nearly fallin off
twice

but i did
and i found the place
where they climbed up
i mean
the people

the hand grips were still there
in the rock
but the log supports
were rotten
no wonder
no one else
wants to do this any more

but i did
and i found the place
where they sat down

cross legged
facing the water
and the sun that heated up the stone
face of the outcrop

thunder and lightning
back in the hills
all happenin at the same time

and every time i closed
my eyes
the heat and amber
washed down
over agawa rock
and every time i closed
my eyes
the heat and amber
washed down
disintegratin
anything that might resemble
a clock

and i saw you late that afternoon

i saw what you were doing
six hundred miles
away
scratchin down those notes

connectin
up with this trance
and i know how it happens

because time and distance
theory don't
work around
here

and i don't suppose
it ever
did

we'll never have to prove it
all
not too many
believe in these ways any more
and nobody's
left here anyway

to tell about anything
except me

and only the spirits
wander around
down at agawa
shore

south of burrard street

where
the people
wander

black
and broken
trudging
between
thirty storey towers
and flop houses

south
of burrard street

rain
comin down
on everyone
draggin along

and i come to you mountain
and i'm talkin
to you

standin
all around
the ocean shore

summit
eyes buried
and sealed
in the clouds

and i'm talkin
to you
mountain

i'm askin
you
where
is your power

and why
can't you
bring the people
home

why can't you bring them home
in your beauty
now

and why
can't you
look down here
just once
just this
once and
get me
off
this

cross

sorcery and power

you
once told me
i had power
and said nothing

i knelt
before the mountain
it had power
and said nothing

i wept
at the ocean shore
it had power
and said nothing

i reached for the sky
it had power
and said nothing

you were
right
about
the power

but both you and i
know about
sorcery
power

yet
after all
this time

we
still
say nothing

another form of art

only beauty
knows
how to wait
in elegance

the rest of us know nothing at all

the big bellied man
knows nothing about waiting
she won't
let him stand
in the coffee line up
and chases him away
even though the flight's
not for another hour

and the cabby who knows nothing about waiting
too impatient
and nervous
wanting not to wait any more
but only to go so
speeds away

and the impetuous
sixteen year old
in the aisle
breasts bouncing around
every time she spins
doing some kind of a freakish ballet
knowing nothing at all about waiting

and you
swish by
silk skirt rustling
against your thigh
caressing the airport air
with some mountain fragrance
i like

and the old woman
who truly knows
how to camouflage waiting
dumps the entire
contents of her bag
on the counter
so the flight attendant
can help her look for a
boarding pass
inciting the entire line up

and the children
who never heard anything
about waiting
not being part of their
repertoire
busier than any
short order cook
at noon time
in just standing still

and only
beauty knows how to wait
in elegance
while the rest of us
squirm
at her feet
nervous and homely
knowing nothing
at all
about waiting
not having ever
been properly
introduced
to this
form of art

turbines and steel

turbines and steel
push me
now

on to the plain
and two
cities

where
the people
meet

along the junction
and rivers fly
five

miles high on
turbines and
steel

don't fail me now
where clouds
stare

at me and don't ever
let this
blue

this blue wash
down and
don't

ever let me
don't ever
let

me free now
a woman
and

child

wait
for me

down at college park

i'm really
back in the saddle
tonight

back on the street
and thinking
of you

down college park way
with some old
time song
and line

i heard on a street
car that didn't
look much like
the back forty
although
i liked the colour

there's really no
resemblance
to the big blue

nite falling down
right beside
the towers
and all around

i never used to be
scared of the dark
but i can
hardly think
hardly think of
another day
without
you

passes right
in front
of me
and the nite
rides away
down
down at college
park

without
you

all the way down

dusty sun lite

creeps
along
between these towers

and gets
me down
to
reforma

boulevard
and the
palm
trees

i really
don't know
what
i'm doin here
without
you
again

we talked
late
last
night

about
the darkness
and the spaniards

again
walking
the street
right
through

right
down
to reforma

again
and all
the way
down

to you

willow and lite

orange
gold
pale
yellow
lite

the
green

the
turquoise

and blue

in the sand

i once
saw a sunset
from four
miles
high

saw love
and
a stranger's

eye

shining
and shining
and walked
through
the nite

and
followed
you down
down
to

to willow
willow
and

lite

voices

i
hear

voices
everywhere

now speak
and whisper

along the valley floor

wolf blinks
in the night
and
stares at
me and
jet streams

talk
to the cloud
swirling
all in time
and whisper
to the great whisper
to the great river

drum
speaking
and pounding
in my heart
beats
like a turbine
beats
like a turbine

turning
in the sky
world
in front
of me
taking me home

again
and again
and again

to you

and hearin
the voices

i know
i'm not losing
it

but i can hear
the
voices
speaking
and whispering
everywhere
everywhere

i go now

the bell of saint john

ten
o'clock
now

and the bell rings
off trinity hill
where you

used to walk
down to St Paul's
sunday
morning
and
i never planned
to be down here
and so now
i'm
only trying
to catch up
to those places
you've already been

hearing
the bell
the bell
of saint john
and
catchin up
catchin up
to those places
you've
already
been

storm dancer

sun
falls
down

in front
of you
and cloud

gathers up
darkness
your hand
reachin out
out to where
the thunder
crackles up from
the horizon
starts to run

and dances
dances
a wild kind
of jig
bobbin around
with a crazy
wind its
partner
howlin
and dippin

black hair
flyin
everywhere

until you
become the dancer
again
storm dancer
climbin
around in the
lightnin
and thunder
drum poundin
everywhere

until
there's no
difference
any more
you can't
tell any more
difference
between the black
storm dancer
and raven

flyin
and flyin
and crashin
and flyin
in the wind
and rain

sierra blue

sierra blue
eyes
in the rain

were all
i could
think
of

that
morning

in taxco

sun
washing
down

thru
the
streets
and stone

and

i never
wept
like
that
for
anyone
before
ever

suncatcher

i
never
knew
you
believed

in
any
of this

but
now
i know you
do

catchin
the sun
right
in your
hand
like
that

entranced
until
i

couldn't
just couldn't

look
away

any
more

and
i don't
know
how i
could ever
could ever

live
with
out
you
now

for w.h. new

good
to have
you along
on this campaign

bill

and i'm glad
you met
the people
on your way down

there
is one thing
you oughtta know

though

and
i'm sorry
to have to be
the one to tell
you

but here it is
you see

we're
not taking
any prisoners

this time around

bein in charge nd all

i never
held
you responsible
for my happiness

or any of those
other
simple
pleasures

of life

i guess
that's why
it kinda
took me by
surprise

you know

i mean decidin
to be in charge
and all that
and you becomin
solely
responsible
for my

misery

silver and clay

my hands are
gettin a
lot

steadier now

and i can work
most every
nite

lately til dawn

and i have
a new
address
down here
at the corner
of reforma
and bay

you know

i never really
changed
much

of anythin

and i'm still
workin
for you
here

still workin
with silver
with

silver

and
sorcerer's
clay

nobody sleeps at nite any more

the soles

of
my
feet

are black

with
ashes

from
this
augury

sun
scorchin

and blazin
along
the horizon

streets and fire
eruptin into
flames

burnin
and burnin
my face

and
eyes

and here

at the corner
of mountain
and sky

nobody
hardly
sleeps
at nite

any more

yaqui desert

back
in the desert

sidewinder

shot
in
the mouth

squirms

rattle
still shakin

i can't believe
what i saw
here
everybody
packin it up
and pullin out
like that

they said
this expedition
never
went
right

from the start

anyway

just about anything

i
used to
approach women

solely

on my good
looks

when
that failed
i tried writing

i heard it
said
somewhere
before

that
desperate
people
will
try

just
about
anything

silver and rain

if ever i needed you
the silver and rain
ever needed you
needed you now
and once again i said
i needed you all through the nite
the earth and stars and earth start again
all through the nite if i ever said
i needed you all nite long
and laid down my song and
i laid down my song for you
and oceans emptied out and emptied
all the tides ran down ran down along the sea
there isn't any return now there isn't any at all
any return to this wind and rain
and in my dreams i saw you saw you once again
there isn't a time of day now
not any time of day there isn't any moment
now when i don't think of you
when i don't think of you and stars
these stars can't count my love for you
can't count love for you any more
these stars can't count any more love
or any day now can count the stars for you
without my dreams a long way into the nite
you know that i would
you know that i would do anything
at all once again and you needed me and
if i ever needed you needed you

once again i would i would need you
all the forever time i would need you
time forever and time and needed
and if i ever needed you and if i
ever said i needed you now
there's nothing left but now
there's nothing left but
nothing left now but
silver and rain

proclamations and dust

some day now
i'll
write that great
monumental song
for you
you know the kind
angelic trumpet pronouncements
that stop desert armies
in their tracks
encompass love
and passion
down through the ages
heralded
right through toltec
arches and dreams
adorned with quetzal
armoury and jaguar rings
and i'll throw in
ed's old sorcerer
the wizard statue
for that magical touch
prism lites
and amethyst
floating around
in some kind of a medicine dreamer's
cosmic hallucination
maybe drag
in those eclectic harpsichords
for grandeur and pomp
i'll call in every marker
i ever had from all the
songwriters i ever knew
to put this one together

you'll probably
think it's the end
of the world
and i'll make
sure raven's
there waving
those old songs
and myths
around like
some kind of national flag
flapping crazily in a dusty wind
storm banging
around clouds
and heavens
and i'll make
sure it happens
at the mountain's breast
all in beauty

seeking
raw
power's
proclamation
of what i see
what i see
in your
willow eyes
your willow eyes
and soul

for jeannette

let me

whisper
in your
ear

how

beautiful
you
are

tonight

let me
touch
your
okanagan
beauty

just
this
once

and when

i return
to these
hungry
streets

again

exuding
breath
and pain

let me

whisper
in your
ear

how

beautiful
you
are

tonight

norman, oklahoma

rainy days

two
cans of coke
rattle on the dash
while harrison and orbison
wail at about 90
decibels each
trying to cover
up the sound
of rain pounding
on my windshield
wipers flailing
around crazily
to their own kind
of deranged beat
coming down the highway
full tilt on a monday afternoon
i don't like being hurled
around in a storm like this
any more than you do
although i know you're not too
impressed these days
with my antics and what
happened this summer
down at montreal river
getting fully certified
and such i guess i don't
really know what
to say much any more either
so i just hold you
and hope you can imagine
something like perfect love
like maybe you could imagine
how the morning holds the mist
in her arms or something like that

or maybe
i could train myself
train myself to love you
like lovers do on warm summer nights
or maybe i could learn
some of those magician
tricks i could do to impress you
but i'm not going to change my stance any
on what i saw down there
not changing it at all
cos i don't see them together
that often any more
eagle and raven
i mean
flying between
the sun spots
like that will never
really go down in history
as any kind of hallucination
going on to get fully certified
insane about

down the fast lane

gettin
dragged
down the fast lane
once again and comin
all the way from new orleans
that night floatin along
at about 40000 feet and
makin that jump to
over five hundred mph
now as we crawl
into town with the sun
already dissolved somewhere
tired and fed up with all this
slow down and no you can't land
yes you can land
better wait another hour
better get back to buffalo
better get back now
to the other side of the lake
and better get this bird down captain
before you run outta
jet fuel smells like hell
you know at least i'm travellin
pretty light now cos my luggage
is gone off maybe to a new york
city skyline silhouette
laffin out loud with
some kind of grotesque arms
reachin out to grab one last stop
i knew we shouldn't a touched
down and give any baggage handler
one more chance to throw my suitcase
down on the tarmac
from the top of that conveyor

belt fitted with that perfect
openin beside the steel buffer
that just manages to clutch
the handle slitherin by and
guts the leather case open
like a deer's belly bein
bled after the kill
in the morning and
i wouldn't want to be a bag
or something like that
down there cos
i'm not that tough
only another hour to wait
but my face is burnin
about as hot as it's gonna get any more
waitin for the light to take over
for the silver to take hold
for the conjurin to start
and then you slide down
down into that sorcerer's pit
of wild stars and ice hangin from the walls
everywhere and raven cracklin on a perch
made of pure oak and aged elm
in this smoky dungeon
black and trim
and skiddin
through this corridor
is not too much different than gettin dragged
down the fast lane
once again

at allison pass

mountains
grow
along
the trail

and
climb

a slow sky
path
to

crow's nest
float and
drift

where
eagle
and
raven

sail
through
clouds

turn and face the wind

and mist
haunt
me
now

like
some shaman's
dream
rising
along side
these earthly trees
reaching for the peak

your voice and spirit
everywhere
now

if only i could
have you
here

but summits
wash
away

ascend
and
slowly

ascend
slowly
now

and
slowly
ascend
ascend
and rise
away

earth walk talks

i heard
you took that long ride
out to clouds and sky and blue
heavens around you now
all finished up with
this earth walk
it was a good one Tom
and i'm really glad
we met those times
coming in from around
all ends of this country
talking about the work
we did and sort of keeping
everyone straight on things
i can still see you talking
and smiling and talking
the earth walk talk
even here
at coquihalla peaks
between clouds
and blue and shaman's mist
really needing
to be kept straight
and don't worry Tom
i'll be keeping
an eye on things
til i run into
you again
and remain
your friend
always
wayne

Spirit Warrior Raven
Dream Winter

A long time ago, in the land of the Anishnawbe, there was a man. His name was Raven and he was a great spirit warrior. I met the Raven man early one summer, not far from where our people came to fish in the spring. He had come a long way and was hungry and very tired, so I asked him to share my fire and food.

As we sat by the campfire, neither of us spoke. I prepared a small meal of fresh game over the open fire. We ate in silence and gave thanks to the animal spirits for the food we took that evening. Finally, I spoke to the Raven man.

"You have been away a long time, Raven. It is good that you came back," I said, as I watched for his reaction.

The Raven man closed his eyes and took a deep breath, then gazed into the flames of the campfire.

"I have passed through a Dream Winter," he said in a weary voice.

"Do you know of this land?" he asked.

I replied that I was not a shaman, but had heard of such a place. I said that I knew it was a spirit world and that it was not a safe place to be.

"I had been in a great battle and suffered many wounds when I marched through the Dream Winter," the Raven man went on.

"After travelling for many days I began to feel that I could no longer go on. I didn't know where I was any more or where I was travelling.

"I stopped to rest against a great pine tree on the trail. The wound in my shoulder had started to bleed again and I felt dizzy. I tried to listen for any sound of life around me but heard nothing. There were no sounds. Yet I knew that here, in the great forests and hills of our people, the air should be bristling with the clatter of birds and small animals, a noisy red squirrel, an indignant marten. But, I heard nothing, only a graveyard of silence.

"Snow fell down in enormous flakes and settled quietly on the spruce and balsam branches. The sky hung overhead like a solemn grey blanket. Damp and cold. The small valley I had entered was shrouded in heavy winter mist. There was no breeze to sway the boughs of the wintergreen trees. Only stillness."

The Raven warrior shook his head, trying to dislodge the trance he was in. Maybe it was the loss of blood and his hunger that had robbed him of his senses. He had not eaten for many days and he was weak. Too weak to go on. His strength was drained as he slumped beside the thick pine tree where he tried to rest. He began to shiver with the cold and couldn't contain himself as his whole body began to shake. He fell to the ground and into unconsciousness.

Several hours passed before he felt the icy snow melting on his face. He struggled to pull himself up to a sitting position, using the pine tree as his backrest, and stared out across the small stream that ran quietly beside him. Two huge boulders squatted across the creek and seemed familiar, but he couldn't remember why. His head fell back as he tried to remember. The rock formation was important, but why...... why...... Then, suddenly he remembered.

He slowly pulled himself to his feet and lunged across the stream, stumbling and falling as the icy water soaked his leggings and arms. There would be a cache between the stones. He remembered his people again and the winter caches they made. It was the custom of his people, during good times, to prepare a cache of stores containing food and weapons and bury them in a stone mound where they could be found at a later time.

He pawed through the snow, prying the mound and pulling the frozen earth loose with his hands. Finally, he could feel the pelt and grew frantic as he tried to get it free. He reached beside him and broke a dead limb from a fallen tree and scraped the heavy hide that held the stores he needed and jerked it open.

The pungent odour of the cured meat flared his nostrils as he ravenously tore huge chunks from the dried strip. He satisfied his hunger until he could swallow no more.

The Raven warrior removed the cache and again crossed the creek. There was better shelter on the other side and he brought the cache of supplies to a rock crevice where the entrance was well-protected by several large spruce trees. The long boughs had helped keep the snow away and he had little work to prepare a small campsite.

He soon opened the bundle of stores retrieved from the stone cache. Inside the heavy moose hide, the supplies were covered in a great lynx wrap.

He opened the wrap to examine its contents. There was a plentiful supply of goods wrapped in the fur. Besides the dried meat, there was flint for fire, two flint knives, several arrowheads, leather thongs for binding and sinew for a bow.

Raven opened a small pouch he found in the cache. There were several packets of herbs, a small silver medallion and a beautiful eye of turquoise. This was the medicine bag of Blue Star, a stone worker of his people. Raven smiled as he reached for his own medicine bag, only to find that it was gone. He thought for a moment and knew it must have been lost in the great battle with the plains warriors. His face darkened as he again thought of his loss and was silently grateful for the medicine bag Blue Star had concealed in the cache.

The Raven warrior made a small campfire that evening. He pulled the great lynx fur around his shoulders, sitting cross legged and erect as he meditated. He drew large breaths from the air, calming himself until he could feel his muscles relax. He gave thanks to the people and man above until he began to hear the drum. With each breath the drumbeat grew louder until his whole being became filled with the spirit of his people. He summoned their strength in the trance-like state, pulling the silver light from the crown of his head down through his body. Again he gave his gratitude for the cache he had found. He drew the silver light up again. This time up the outside of his body to join above his head and then down through the centre of his body. He drew the light until it flowed easily and seemed to fill him with energy and strength.

As darkness came, the Raven warrior passed from trance to sleep beside the dying embers of his campfire, and slipped into a medicine dream.

……….. he stood on a cloud as white as the winter snows. He could no longer see the earth and knew he was in the world above. The sky around him was as brilliant as the electric blue of a turquoise stone. He felt like he was floating. His entire body glistened and radiated a magical silver aura.

He heard the great mystery speak. His voice sounded very quiet and seemed to surround him.

"Raven warrior, you have had many battles. Many of the people have never returned from the battle with the plains warriors and many have suffered mortal wounds. They still carry their wounds into the valley of life where they remain hideously crippled even though they still live."

The great mystery was silent for a moment, then spoke again.

"Your journey is not yet complete, and you must heal before you go on. Follow the creek until it joins the river. Here you will meet a woman. She is called the Willow Woman. She will help you to remember the people again and who you are. This Dream Winter land you are in is not a kind land and some have found death here. Go now, Raven warrior, and remember what I have said."

The Raven warrior awoke and found it was morning. He could not remember what land he was in. He thought he was in the north country, but the snows kept melting as soon as they fell. It was a dreary land and the sun seemed never to shine.

He remembered the dream and that he should go to the place where the creek met the river. He couldn't recall why he was to go there, but started his journey. His legs felt heavy as he trudged through the wet snow. The dampness chilled him and he shook with the cold whenever he stopped to rest.

The silence was unnerving in this Winter Dream land as the great mystery had called it. There was no sound of any game or wind or tree creaking in the breeze. The mist hung heavy and grey along the stream he followed. The silence seemed to steal his strength away.

The Raven warrior travelled for several days, dragging himself through the great forest. He followed the stream until he saw the river and fell to one knee to rest, trying to remember why he had come to this place. He was too exhausted and hung his head. he wished the silence would end. He ached for the life he had known in the valley that was his home.

Suddenly he was startled by a voice behind him.

"What do you seek, Raven man?" a woman's voice asked, as calm and still as the land around them.

The Raven warrior turned his head and was blinded by a brilliant light. He lifted his arm to shield his eyes.

"Who are you?" he asked.

"I am called Willow Woman," she replied.

The light began to subside and the Raven warrior could see the face of the woman. The light formed a silver aura around her and shimmered in the air even though there was no sun present. She turned and began to walk to a lodge he had not seen, but was right in the path of the way he had come. He wondered why he had not seen it. She beckoned for him to follow.

The lodge inside was immediately warm and a smokeless cedar fire burned smoothly, giving the interior a golden appearance. The woman spread a small piece of doeskin in front of her as he sat down.

Again she asked him the same question. "What do you seek, Raven man?"

"I seek the valley of life that is my home, but I cannot remember the direction where it might be," he answered.

"You must rest and heal before you continue," she said. "You will find your homeland soon, but first you must rest."

The Willow Woman removed his shirt and began to wash his wounds with the cloth. The ointment she used was a golden colour and the wounds would disappear each time she bathed them with the cloth.

The Raven warrior was astonished as he watched her work.

"What magic is this that you make here, Willow Woman?" he asked.

"The magic comes from your own power, Raven. The ointment is a simple one. It is made from the first rain of spring and the liquor drawn from a white birch at dawn. It cools and draws your power to the surface. This is how it heals," she replied as she finished washing the rest of his body. She handed him a shirt, leggings and a breech clout made from the hide of a black deer.

"Now you must seek your spirit animal and renew your strength, Raven," she said as she reached for another pouch that lay beside her.

She emptied its contents in front of her and vigorously rubbed her hands over them for some time. There were four clear crystal stones and she handed them to him.

"These are bitter stones. Place two in each hand before you seek your spirit power. When you have completed this ritual, all your bitterness will remain in the stones. They will turn black if you are a true spirit warrior, Raven. The bitterness and the pain you carry will be locked in these stones forever."

She took down the medicine drum that hung on the wall of her lodge and began to beat it. The drum was small but it was very loud, like a great water drum.

The Raven warrior closed his eyes and listened to the beating drum. He could feel the pounding in his body. His breathing slowed to the drumbeat and he was aware of the blackness for only a second as he slipped into a medicine dream.

.... the night was very dark and the stars bristled over his head. Then, in front of him was the Raven dancer of his people. He began to dance, twisting and turning to the pounding of the drum. At once he heard the singers' booming chant that drove the dancer on. He felt like he was high above the earth. He watched the silver aura trailing from his hand like a ribbon of glistening light. The tiny dreamcatcher he had as a boy hung from a lock of his black hair, sparkling in the silver sheen. A shower of stars fell in front of him and he saw the Willow Woman smile.

He heard his spirit power speak in an echoing voice.

"I am trickster and magician of all the people, Raven. I am your strength and power if you be a true spirit warrior. I will be with you always until we meet here once again."

The Raven man looked up at me and said, "This is how I came to be here. When I looked at the stones in my hands, they had turned as black as the night and so I threw them in the river."

The next morning when I awoke, the Raven warrior had gone.

Spirit Warrior Raven
Emerald Spring

A long time ago, in the land of the Anishnawbe, there was a man. His name was Raven and he was a great spirit warrior. I met the Raven man one night not far from here. He had come a long way and was hungry and needed to rest, so I asked him to share my fire and food.

I prepared a small meal of fresh fish baked over the fire. We ate in silence and gave thanks to the water spirits for the food we took that evening. Finally, I spoke to the Raven man.

"You have been gone a long time, Raven. It is good that we meet again," I said, waiting for his response.

The Raven man's eyes flickered as he looked up at me. "Have you ever seen the land of Emerald Spring?" he asked me smiling.

I was puzzled and replied "No. I am not a shaman and have not heard of such a land. Tell me about this land you speak of."

"I had been travelling many days through a land called the Dream Winter," the Raven man began.

"One morning when I awoke, it had grown very warm, almost like summer. As the day wore on it became very hot and I had to remove my winter garments. Yet, all around me, the land was still in its winter gown. The snow had all melted and the earth was very dry and brown. There was very little run-off from the winter snows and the melting waters seemed to evaporate into the warm wind.

"As I came to a rocky ridge, I could see far into the distance. There was a light haze over the hills and valleys and it seemed to have a shimmering green hue to it. It seemed to be trying to descend on the land. The wintergreens had changed to a glowing emerald green, yet all the other trees were barren and had no spring or summer foliage. The green haze seemed to be suspended in the air just above the highest tips of the birch, poplar and maple trees. There were many places where the grass had turned green, as if some great light had fallen on them. Yet, the shrubs around them looked burnt and brown.

"I descended into a small valley where there was a stream and I knew I would find game. Before too long I found a beaver and shot it with my bow and arrow. As I cooked the beaver, I took some of the herbs from a cache that I had found and used them to season the fresh meat. Shortly after I had eaten I became very drowsy. The land around me began to seem dreamy and I lay down beside my campfire to sleep, even though it was still early in the afternoon.

"I could not tell if I was asleep or awake as I lay by the fire. I could smell the light dampness of spring foliage and thought I stood up and began to walk toward the stream. I could hear a flute playing. It seemed to come across a shallow in the stream where the water was very still.

"As I began to walk across the stream, I was startled. Instead of stepping into the water, I seemed to be floating and walking above it. The stream got wider and wider and I floated until finally I thought I was in the sky. I could no longer tell where the water and sky met. They seemed to melt into each other around the clouds that looked like a blue mist. The sound of the flute still sang in the air and I followed it.

"The water in front of me began to shine as if the midday sun had fallen across it. A great pine tree appeared, as green as the summer forests. I saw a woman standing beside the tree. She was playing the flute and I was drawn towards her. There was an aura around her that sparkled like the shining silver water of the stream.

"She lowered the flute from her lips and smiled as I approached her. I realized then that it was the Willow Woman I had met in the Dream Winter many days before.

"'You have travelled a long way, Raven,' she said. Her voice seemed as soft and silvery as the aura that surrounded her.

"'Few have come this far. This is the spirit land of Emerald Spring and you will find much strength here,' she said, as she turned and began to walk into the forest behind her.

"'You are on the journey of a true spirit warrior,' she said, beckoning me to follow her again.

"As I walked behind her, the air became alive and seemed to breathe. The green-blue colours danced and glistened. I felt like I was swimming in a foamy sea. The air seemed to make us light and we floated towards the forest that shone in the emerald greenness the Willow Woman spoke of.

"She finally came to a small lodge deep within the forest. There was a campfire burning outside the lodge and the sun seemed only to shine through the dense forest in a single ray of light. It beamed through the top of the trees to the spot where the fire burned.

"The Willow Woman sat down beside the fire and motioned for me to join her. As I sat down I couldn't believe the warmth of the sunbeam. It seemed to fill every pore of me and flow through every part of my body. The sweet burning smell of cedar permeated the air and the smoke floated up to the tops of the trees.

"The Willow Woman reached up and began to caress the air with her outstretched arms, drawing it towards her. The air seemed to respond and the shimmering greens of spring pulsed towards her hands and fingers. The colours danced and glistened a thousand shades of green until finally the glowing colours were drawn into a single wave of dark emerald green. The wave grew smaller and smaller until it was no larger than a bean and fell into the Willow Woman's hand.

"She cupped her hand around the tiny fragment of colour, then closed it and drew it to her breast.

"'You have seen the essence of the Emerald Spring, Raven,' she said quietly.

"'Place this in your medicine bag. It is strength beyond your own strength. When you feel you can no longer go on, touch the stone and remember the source from which it came,' she spoke as she reached out and handed it to me.

"The stone had turned to a true forest emerald green and sparkled as if it were alive. I could feel its power and warmth radiating in my hand as I placed it in my medicine bag and drew the string tight.

"The dust from the stone covered the woman's hand. She cupped it into the centre of her palm and flung it into the fire. It erupted into a cloud of smoke as I watched.

"At that moment I found myself wide awake and beside my own campfire. I began to follow the trail we are on and that is how I came to meet you here," the Raven man said.

He loosened the string on his medicine bag and drew out a green coloured stone to show me. It sparkled and glowed in the light. I could feel the warmth and radiance from it.

The next morning when I awoke, the Raven man had gone.

Spirit Warrior Raven
Rainbow Village

A long time ago, in the land of the Anishnawbe, there was a man. His name was Raven and he was a great spirit warrior. I met the Raven man on a mountain overlooking our village. He had come a long way and had stopped to rest before making his way down into our camp.

It had rained that day and we watched a rainbow that appeared over our village. As the rainbow disappeared, the Raven warrior asked "Have you ever seen a village of four rainbows?"

"No, I have not," I answered, and returned his question.

"Have you?" I asked.

"I have only seen it once," the Raven man said.

"I had been travelling for many moons in a land that was far from our village. One night I made camp by a river. The river was black and powerful and ran swiftly through a long deep rock cut. I did not recognize what river it was, but knew it was in the land of our people.

"The pine trees towered far above the water and huge ferns grew in the shade of the lofty trees beside this river. The summer greens shone in the late afternoon sun even though grey clouds moved across the sky. I could smell the dank odour of the summer foliage and it seemed to permeate the breeze high on the rock outcrop where I had camped.

"That evening I sat high on a cliff, just beneath the stone overhang where I had a small fire burning. I thanked the animal spirits for the food I had taken and for the beauty of the land we lived in."

As dusk descended on the land, the Raven warrior shivered in the cool air. He placed a larger log across his campfire while he mended his moccasins that were worn and badly in need of repair. He had been travelling for weeks and had not stopped except to hunt small game for food.

The night grew colder as he slept and he pulled the great lynx wrap tightly around himself. He turned towards the stone face and worked his way tightly into the rock crevice until he was comfortable and shielded from the wind. The fatigue of the day's travel let him sleep quickly while the embers of the burning log reflected against the cliff. The coldness did not waken him as he slipped into a dream.

"..........I stood on top of the cliffs overlooking the river. I wondered how I would cross it. There were no narrows in either direction so I started downstream to look for a safe place to cross.

"As I looked into the sky I was surprised. It had turned a brilliant blue and seemed to shimmer. High in the heavens I saw an eagle. She flew in great circles, descending towards the river. I thought the eagle would dive as it flew nearer to the river. But instead of diving, the eagle began to change its shape. I stared in disbelief. It was no longer an eagle. It changed into a woman right in front of my eyes. I could not remember how long it had been since I had met the woman, for it was the Willow Woman.

"She beckoned me to follow her, so I started to walk towards her. Suddenly I stopped and looked down. The river was far below and I was higher than the tallest pine. I turned to look back. The cliffs I had walked on were far below. I took a deep breath and again looked up.

"The Willow Woman smiled and beckoned me again. When I had almost reached her, she turned and appeared to be flying. I reached out my arms and was immediately beside her. It seemed like we were floating through the air.

"As I looked up I was flooded with a breathtaking display of colours. They flashed and sparkled the full spectrum of the rainbow. Then they began disappearing as quickly as they had started and it became night.

"The Willow Woman pointed below. There was a great desert. It shone in what seemed to be moonlight, but there was no moon in the sky. We slowly descended and landed on the desert sand.

"The Willow Woman turned to me and spoke. 'You seek your homeland, Raven, but I cannot help you. The only one who can help you is the desert coyote. He is here and this is why I have brought you into this night desert,' she said.

"She motioned for me to sit down and disappeared into the darkness.

"I sat on the desert sand gazing around. I was confused and bewildered. I had never seen such a desert and wondered what this desert night would bring. I sat motionless for a long time. Nothing happened. The stillness of the night seemed to calm me as I took several deep breaths. I closed my eyes and waited.

"Suddenly I was startled by a howling screech behind me. I jerked around to see a coyote sitting directly in front of me. My heart began to pound and I shook my head, not believing what I was seeing. The coyote was as large as a man. I winced as the coyote lifted his head again and howled.

"The dog-like creature spoke.

"'Why have you come here to the night desert?' the creature cackled in a mocking voice.

"Before I could answer, the coyote changed into an old and very wrinkled man. I did not recognize any of the markings on the old warrior's shirt.

"The old man practically shouted at me.

"'Have you no tongue with which to speak, Ojibway man!'

"'I seek my homeland!' I blurted out, still astonished with this sight.

"The old man began to chuckle in a raspy voice. Soon he began to laugh. His laughter grew louder and louder until it boomed in the desert night air. The old man held his sides as he shook and continued to laugh for several minutes. Finally he seemed to catch his breath and spoke again.

"'The land you seek is beyond the mountain,' he clucked.

"'Beyond a mountain without any pride,' he said as he began to laugh again.

"The old man sat down and roared in his laughter. Tears began to roll off his cheeks in his hysteria.

"'The mountain has no pass!' he gasped.

"The old man stood up and began to walk away wheezing and coughing as he laughed.

"'The mountain has no pass!' his laughter boomed into the night.

"I awoke the next morning. It had grown very cold. I shook my head, half remembering the dream, and started to make my way downstream.

"I soon came to a shallow narrows on the river. As I waded across, the water was very cold. It was like the spring run-off from the melting snow.

"I stepped on to the shore and looked up. There was a mountain ridge in front of me. It seemed to be endless, yet I somehow knew I had to cross this ridge. I searched for an opening, but saw only steep cliffs and a few trees along the face of the bluffs. I continued my search further downstream.

"Finally, I spotted a likely place to try climbing the ridge. There were several trees growing in a long crevice where I thought I might get up. As I started to climb the face of the ridge, it seemed to grow steeper and steeper. I had to stop to rest several times before I reached a small ledge not far from the top of the ridge.

"As I looked up I saw a great black raven sitting on a small and gnarled pine. His black coat shone in the sun. It sparkled and turned a deep blue, like the blue of late dusk.

"Then suddenly, the raven flew off and I could hear its calling in the distance as I worked myself up the short way to the top of the ridge.

"I followed a slightly worn path a short way and came around a huge rock and looked up. My heart stopped. There below me in the midst of four rainbows was the village of our people.

"I couldn't contain the longing within me from a two winter march. I knelt on one knee to rest. Tears burned in my eyes and my heart wept with joy as I watched the rainbows fade and disappear. I recognized two women walking, Many Fires and Two Moons. A small boy ran along behind them."

The Raven warrior pointed to the stream by our village.

"They walked there by the water," he said.

When I turned back to face him, the Raven warrior had already gone. I could see him far down the trail as he made his way to our camp.